Tony McAuley's Glens

Walking and Cycling in North Antrim

Cottage
Publications

First published by Cottage Publications,
Donaghadee, N. Ireland 2000.
Copyrights Reserved.
Text and Photographs © Tony McAuley & Brian McAuley 2000.
Design © Cottage Publications
Maps based upon the 1992 Ordnance Survey of Northern Ireland
1:50000 Maps 'Larne' and 'Ballycastle'
with the permission of the controller of H.M.S.O
© Crown Copyright Permit No.1548
All rights reserved.
No part of this book may be reproduced or stored on any media
without the express written permission of the publishers.
Design & origination in Northern Ireland.
Printed & bound in Singapore.

ISBN 1 900935 18 X

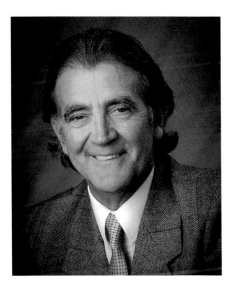

Over the many years that I've known Tony McAuley I've come to associate him with a variety of things. They include broadcasting on radio and television, documentary film making, Irish music, folk song, and spoofing at length about the delights of the Antrim Glens. This book however comes as a surprise for I never knew him to be a dedicated walker, unless he was walking to the bar to order or collect his pint. However, the proof is in these pages which I've read, enjoyed and have learnt a great deal from.

Grab your boots, your walking stick (if you need one) and take to the open air. After reading this, I'm almost tempted to do the same thing myself.

In memory of my father,
William John McAuley
- a Glensman

Contents

Introduction   7

Journeys:

    Carncastle to Glenarm   11
    Carnlough to Waterfoot   19
    Cushendall and Glenariff   29
    Cushendall and Cushendun   39
    Glenaan and Glendun   49
    Cushendall and Newtown-Crommelin   61
    Rathlin Island   71
    Giant's Causeway to Dunseverick   81

Charles McAuley   91

Detachable Route Cards   inside back cover

"The blue hills of Antrim, I see in my dreams,
The high hills of Antrim, the glens and the streams,".
Joseph Campbell

Introduction

My father, William John McAuley

My father was proud to be a Glensman. He was born and reared in the townland of Lubitavish at the foot of Glenaan. My grandfather was originally from Glendun as was his grandfather before him. My grandmother Elizabeth McElheron was reared close by in the townland of Drumfaskey. In addition, my great grandfather had eight sisters all of whom married, thereby reinforcing and enhancing this North Antrim connection, so I can justifiably claim a strong association with one of the loveliest and most historic regions in Ireland. The McAuley name in fact, is one of the oldest in the Glens, and my antecedents for several generations were associated with the townlands of Savagh and Eagle Hill at the high end of Glendun, places with romantic names situated close to sparse and exposed surroundings. They knew hard times and good times. They lived lives that were simple by modern standards, and undoubtedly more austere, but nonetheless fulfiling and complete.

Grandparents Bernard & Elizabeth McAuley

The McAuleys like their neighbours, were hill farmers, sturdy members of a community bonded by a common culture, a shared faith, and a lifestyle characterised by forbearance, hardship and endurance. The quality and the

My father (standing foreground) with two brothers and three sisters.

pace of life in Glendun and the other Glens altered scarcely at all over the years, but change has been rapid of late and the communities are now much smaller, less cohesive. The customs and civilities that bound them are not as apparent as they used to be. The wider world has impacted upon the traditional culture of the Glens to such an extent that it is now almost extinct. Most of the men and women who experienced life in those simpler times have passed on, but those that I knew I remember with affection. They looked upon me as one of their own and I take some pride in that. I only wish I had taken time to know them better.

The renowned natural beauty of the Glens is self evident, and thankfully largely unspoiled. They remain unique, welcoming and special, but the decline in farming, the lack of alternative local employment, the rising cost of housing and some bizarre planning decisions have all been detrimental. Glens folk however have always been resilient. They know the unique value of what surrounds them; they are proud of their place and of its past, and they know that given time and attention the Glens of Antrim will continue to flourish.

I would not have considered writing this book were it not for the pioneering endeavours of others whose knowledge of the area was matched by their affection. The various journals of the excellent Glens of Antrim Historical Society, 'The Glynns' were an invaluable source of reference, as

My parents on their wedding day.

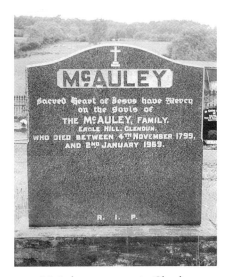

McAuley gravestone in Glendun

were many of its other publications, and in particular 'Oh Maybe It Was Yesterday' edited and compiled by three outstanding local historians, Malachy McSpar-ran, Cahal Dallat and Jimmy Irvine. Cathal Dallat's book 'A Personal View' served as a role model as did the late Jack McBrides 'Traveller in the Glens.'

I was most capably assisted throughout by my son Brian who lives and works in the Glens. He is an outdoor educa-tion instructor and he knows the topography intimately. He supplied much of the text and helped take many of the accompanying photographs. He was supportive throughout and the knowledge he acquired as a result of his work in and around the Glens area was invaluable. He was enthusi-astic and helpful in every possible way. It is fitting that he has returned to reside close to the hills and valleys where his forefathers once lived and worked. I think they would approve of that.

There are eight routes covered within these pages. Two of them cross mountain country where there are no proper roads and so they can only be covered on foot. The remainder, with the exception of the Giant's Causeway route, could be cycled for much of the way. Each walk is lengthy but each one can be made shorter. My selection was made on the basis of variety and my wish to combine the beauty of landscape with the wealth of local history. My choice was also determined by the necessity of respecting rights of way as well as those of the peo-ple whose land is their livelihood. I hope I have chosen routes that are challenging but worthwhile, strenuous but fulfiling and

My son Brian as a child (above) and me as a child (below)

rewarding. In particular I hope that this modest endeavour will in some way contribute to the readers knowledge of the Glens of Antrim, an area that is very much a part of my past and my present life.

"An rud a líonas an tsúil lionann sé an croí ."
- What fills the eye also fills the heart.

Carncastle to Glenarm

Looking down on Ballygalley Head

This walk begins in the small village of Carncastle which lies on the inland road that runs between Ballygalley and Glenarm. Carncastle is beautifully situated. It faces the sea with a traditional pattern of fields gently rising toward the Antrim Plateau. There is a feeling of tranquillity about Carncastle that is seldom disturbed. It has the attributes of a village. It is surrounded by farmland, but it is situated within ten miles of the busy town and port of Larne. It may not be a place of importance but a man of some importance was born in the locality.

David Manson was one of the great pioneers of education in Ireland in the 18th century, yet few people have heard of him, even in teaching circles. Manson's early life was limited in quality. He suffered from rheumatic fever, from which he never really recovered. By way of compensation, he took to learning and eventually he became a teacher in Ballycastle where he married a Miss Lynn. Manson moved to live and work in Belfast where he formed his own independent school in 1754, at Clugson's Entry, now Lombard Street, 'teaching by way of amusement English grammar, reading and spelling at a moderate expense.'

Manson later moved to larger premises in Rosemary Street. He evolved a method of teaching that was ahead of its time insofar as it was play centred. Children were motivated rather than driven, encouraged to advance at their own pace, praised rather than blamed. These were teaching methods that were considered revolutionary in their day. He devised his own spelling and reading books, encouraged inventiveness and creativity, and he referred to his institution as 'the play school.' He saw his work as play and wanted his pupils to enjoy learning in the same way. Among his pupils were a young brother and sister destined to play their own significant part in the turbulent history of Belfast in the 1790s; Mary Anne McCracken and her unfortunate brother Henry Joy who was hanged in Belfast for his involvement in the rebellion of 1798.

Leaving the village, this route follows the Ballycoose Road to the left which leads up into the hills. It continues to rise, providing views of the coastline and surrounding landscape. To the south, the view is dominated by the steep-

The pub at Carncastle

sided walls of Sallagh Braes. These form an impressive natural amphitheatre that dwarfs the surrounding landscape. There is a rath in a field on the right, one of several in the vicinity, and just one of the many thousands scattered throughout Ireland. People frequently refer to these earthen raths as 'forts' in the belief that they were defensive sites of some importance. Although relatively few have been excavated, the evidence collected suggests that the vast majority were used for domestic purposes. Most raths are 'univallate' and consist of a single earthen ring and ditch. Others have several rings, 'multivallate', and are more elaborate. They may have been places of ritual assembly or inauguration of some kind. It may be that others with several rings were erected by people of importance. Raths in general are still places of mystery, but it is fairly certain that they served a variety of functions, including the protection of cattle against the elements and against raiders. Others were lived in, and some contained several dwellings as well as animal shelters. There are of course legendary raths situated in places like Tara and Navan, but the archaeological evidence indicates that the majority of raths served a basic domestic function despite our desire to associate them with heroic adventures and the epic exploits of great men.

Knock Dhu with Larne in the distance

This entire area has signs of early man's presence. The landscape is dotted with raths, cairns and enclosures. There was much to offer early man here, - access to the sea, fertile land and an abundance of flint. The main rock around Sallagh Braes is limestone, which often contains flint, an ideal material for the construction of primitive tools. It is com-

mon enough for flint implements such as arrow heads, scrapers and knives still to be found, especially in recently tilled fields.

About a mile along the Ballycoose Road there is a car park to the south of which there stands a promontory fort known as Knock Dhu. Promontory forts are commonly found on rocky coasts where the action of the sea or ice has left high mountain spurs, surrounded on three sides by sloping ground or cliffs. Access to the fort would have been hindered by a series of ditches, often built like stone walls, which could be easily defended. Many of these early forts are believed to date from Neolithic times.

Standing Stone

Mountain Solitude

The mountain route, which follows a section of the Ulster Way begins at a stile on the other side of the road. The path soon gives way to open ground. Each fence and wall has a stile over it to allow access, and the views are spectacular, not only those of Knock Dhu and the Antrim coast, for the coastline of Ayrshire, Arran and Kintyre in Scotland can be seen in fine weather. The town, port and Lough of Larne are visible and the ferries that sail in and out of Larne provide additional interest.

The town was named after a prehistoric chieftain called Latharna and Larne Lough was known in earlier times as Ulfrek's Lough. It contains a prominent gravel spit, upon which the remains of Olderfleet Castle can be found. This was the spot where Edward Bruce, brother of Robert the Bruce landed in 1315 when he invaded Ireland in search of a kingship for himself. He was subsequently crowned, but his invasion eventually failed and Bruce never returned home to Scotland. He was killed in battle and his body is buried at Faughart in Co Louth.

The small island known as Ailsa Craig or Paddy's Milestone lies on the horizon. Closer to hand are what look like two large battleships. These are the Maidens - two smaller islands with their lighthouses. One of the lighthouses is derelict. The other like all other lighthouses on this coast is unmanned but is still in use. The twin towers which were built almost half a mile apart were called the East and the West Tower, and they provided a visibility of some fourteen miles. The original lights were first lit in 1829, and the lighthouses were occupied. The rocks on which they stand are small and living out there on the Maidens can't have been easy, for despite their proximity to the land they would have been totally cut off in high winds and stormy weather. The engineer in charge of Irish lights observed in 1899 that if there was ever a problem with the lights *"it could be several days before assistance reached the Maidens."*

The route, marked by the Ulster Way signs, leads to another feature of early man's presence in the area – a standing stone, sometimes known as a gallaun. There are a number of theories as to what these standing stones were used for, and much folklore and romantic theorising has

The hills above Glenarm

Triangulation Point on Black Hill

been generated as a result. Many standing stones are actually recent additions to the landscape, erected as rubbing stones for cattle, or as romantic conceits placed there by landowners. Those stones which actually do date from Neolithic times and later, seem to have served two main purposes. It is believed that they may have been placed in position to mark the way to specific settlements or grazing grounds. The other widely held theory is that they were forerunners of the gravestone, marking a burial site that was in a some way significant. Some authorities maintain that these uprights were placed in the ground to 'anchor' stone walls that subsequently collapsed and were either covered in earth and peat or carted away. Many of these stones still stand defiantly, left these out of superstition or respect when a stone circle or a chambered grave was removed.

The Ulster Way heads inland for a short section through wet boggy ground. It is here that a good pair of walking boots prove their worth. It leads to the highest part of the walk, the triangulation pillar on Black Hill. Care needs to be taken at this point. Mist can very quickly move in and disorientate the walker and the markers for the Ulster Way are difficult to find, even in the best of conditions. They lie to the north east. The path now descends and leads

The Village of Glenarm

Left: The Vennel,
Centre: The Village ,Right: BarbicanGate

through a field full of whin bushes. Soon the land levels out and the path joins the road, above the village of Glenarm.

Glenarm has a charm befitting its age and it is reckoned to be one of the oldest villages in Ireland. It was granted a charter by King John (1199-1216), and as a result it can claim to have existed long before most other towns and villages. The Earls of Antrim have resided in Glenarm since 1682, and the castle with its stout walls and high towers overlooking the river, gives the place much of its character.

A stile allows access onto the road, which descends towards the village, affording views of the glen and the estate of the Earl of Antrim. The road soon divides in two and the route takes us off the main road on to the smaller one on the left. This road is steep and runs along the edge of Glenarm forest, passing the entrance to the forest and eventually entering the small village.

The church of St Patrick, standing on the shoreward side of the village, was built in 1763 on the site of an old Fran-

narm is not nearly as busy as it might be. There has been much talk of the village getting a well deserved 'make over' and this would go a long way towards reviving its fortunes.

ciscan Abbey. It is a local tradition that the headless body of Shane O'Neill (Shane the Proud) is buried nearby. The harbour on the other side of the picturesque river was once among the busiest on the East coast. In the seventeenth century it contained a shipbuilding yard capable of building a vessel of some forty tons. More recently, large quantities of limestone were shipped across to Scotland and England. The limestone was quarried locally. The quarrying which began in the late 18th century provided employment and there was an air of industry and enterprise about the village and harbour, especially when the small boats were being loaded with their cargo at the now deserted quayside. Despite its quaint charm and its previous importance, Gle-

Carnlough to Waterfoot

Carnlough Harbour

Many visitors to the Coast Road know Carnlough as a place to stop, stretch their legs and have some lunch before continuing along the coast north to Cushendall, Ballycastle and Portrush or south to Larne and Belfast. In so doing they miss a village of character and charm. It provides an opportune place from which to access the Garron Plateau, a wild blanket bog, the importance of which has been recognised and designated as an Area of Special Scientific Interest. The beauty and importance of the stretch of mountain country lying between Carnlough and Glenariff, part of the old parish of Ardclinis, has been commented on as far back as 1832. In the Ordnance Survey of that year Lieutenant John Taylor wrote;

"Nature has done everything to render the appearance and scenery of this parish romantic and interesting, and to nature alone it is indebted for all it's charms. The peaceful and romantic valley of Glenariff, bounded on either side by lofty and precipitous hills surmounted by a wall of basalt and partially wooded, has no rival in the north in wildness or beauty. This, along with it's coast...have united to render this parish among the most interesting on this most interesting coast."

The walk begins outside one of the focal points of Carnlough - the Londonderry Arms Hotel, once a beautiful old coaching house and now a comfortable modern hotel. It has lost none of its charm. It was owned for a while by Winston Churchill and it was built by his Great Grandmother, Lady Frances Anne Vane Tempest, Marchioness of Londonderry. She was born in London in 1800, her mother was the Countess of Antrim and her father a man of considerable wealth, owning coal mines in the North of England. An only child she inherited his fortune when he died in 1813. She subsequently married Lord Charles Stewart, some twenty three years her senior, one of the Stewart family of Mount Stewart, an elegant, spacious 'great house' on the

shores of Strangford Lough. She also inherited 1000 acres of land lying between Glenarm and Cushendall from her mother, and in 1846 she set about developing Carnlough.

The hotel, was originally built to provide her with a residence on her visits to the area. She built herself a magnificent summer retreat overlooking the sea at Garron Point which is now the well-known St. MacNissi's School.

Carnlough owes a lot to Lady Londonderry for she built not only the coaching house, but Drumalla House on the

Londonderry Arms Hotel

south of the village. In keeping with the custom observed by so many of her class at the time, Lady Londonderry was mainly an absentee land owner. The house accommodated her estate manager and his family. It is now an Outdoor Education Centre run by the Belfast Education and Library Board and it provides environmental and field studies for schools of all kinds.

Lady Londonderry also supported the construction of the small harbour and promoted development of the local quarry industry. In addition she provided aid for the area during the Famine period by importing corn from England and giving employment to the local people through her building programme. She saw to it that there was no rent owing on land where the dreaded potato blight had struck, and she tirelessly raised money in England for Famine relief.

The attractive and sheltered harbour in Carnlough was constructed out of the white limestone quarried from the hills behind. It was completed in 1855, and fittingly the Countess was the first person to land there.

The road opposite the harbour leads away from the village and the bay. Further along this thoroughfare there is a municipal car park and the entrance to a small pathway.

The path leading away from Carnlough

This is where the walk proper begins. Ahead are the prominent white cliffs of Creggan and Gortin Quarries. Rock has been removed from this area since as early as the 1700s but work at the quarries stopped in the 1960s. The path is now part of the Ulster Way and it is a 'way marked' route that leads to Waterfoot.

The path meets with a private road above the site of what was once a well-known youth hostel. At this point the route leads to the right but anyone with time to spare should take the path in front and visit Cranny Falls, one of the most beautiful waterfalls in the Glens. The walk takes a

Cranny Falls

mere ten minutes.

As the trail ascends, it divides again and the correct route is indicated by an Ulster Way signpost. These posts appear every few hundred metres. They do not however provide a fail safe method of navigation so knowledge of how to use a map and compass is recommended. The roadway runs past a local farmers house and then on to a farm track.

Among the major features of this area are its fine dry-stone walls. Some stand up to five feet in height, testimony to the effort and exertion once required to clear and ready this land. The walls were constructed from the stones which had previously littered the ground nearby. The Ulster Way crosses these walls by way of

A lake on the plateau.

a series of wooden stiles which make useful viewing platforms.

Ahead lie two prominent hills known as Big Trosk and Little Trosk. The small valley between the two provides access onto the bogland of the Garron Plateau via a gate at the top. A sign on this gate, hung there by the Carnlough Anglers Club, advises the would be fisherman to return to the hotel and purchase a permit, for this is also an area popular with anglers. The plateau is littered with lakes of varying sizes which the local angling club stocks on a regular basis.

As the walk continues, evidence of human impact on the environment becomes less evident and there is a growing sense of isolation in this wild open area, a real sense of being separate and alone on the wide blanket bog that covers the entire plateau. Other people are rarely seen. The bogland consists of peat, which is of course nothing more than partially decayed plant material. The material of the bog is inhibited from decaying down due to the relatively low temperatures experienced on this plateau. Moreover the high rainfall keeps it waterlogged for most of the year. As a result of the

An Ulster Way Stile

inhospitable conditions on the bog, only specialised and highly adapted plants and animals can survive.

Two particular plants exemplify this. The observant walker will spot both in abundance. These are the Sundew and the Butterwort. These plants find that the bog cannot provide all the nutrients they need and so they supplement their intake by trapping the plentiful supplies of insects that thrive in the moisture. As the insects decay, the nutrients from their bodies are absorbed by the plant, allowing it to persevere in the most difficult of conditions. The Butterwort in particular is well suited to its habitat. It also possesses the ability to digest the pollen and heather that land on its leaves, providing it with nitrogen.

The Sundew is one of those plants imbued with medicinal qualities by old lore. It was believed that the dew from the plant could cure warts, corns and even help sunburn. Other plants seen on the plateau include various species of rare orchid, heather, cottongrass and purple moorgrass. There is also an abundance of rushes, which grow abundantly in tufts on badly drained ground.

Rushes at one time had an important function in Ireland and elsewhere. They were gathered in bunches, Summer and early Autumn. The green outer skin was peeled away to expose the pith and they were then dipped in melted lard or fat and allowed to dry. The rushes were then used as

*Wild
flowers*

Mountain Rushes

even stumble across nests hidden deep down in the tufts of grass that are scattered over the bog. The wet conditions are also ideal for amphibians and it is common for the walker to notice frogs frantically hopping out of the way. The more observant might even sight a newt, a rare and endangered animal. Herds of wild goat also live on this wide and open landscape. When conditions are bad on the plateau they can often be seen at lower levels, for they sometimes leave their mountain home to search for food.

The walker needs to be well kitted out for crossing the plateau. The weather can change at a moments notice, and waterproofs, good boots and some food are as important as a map and compass. A small pair of binoculars is a useful addition.

Along the plateau other interesting sites appear if the weather is favourable. To the north there is a solitary hill with a cairn on top. This is known as Turnley's Seat. Francis Turnley was another of the prosperous landowners to have lived in the Glens and it was he more than any other who

candles, 'rushlights' that burned with a clear, steady flame. Several well placed rushlights would illuminate an average small cottage, and this simple method of lighting by rushlight was in use for thousands of years.

Irish Hare, Buzzards, Hen Harrier, Red Grouse and Dunlin may also be spotted on the plateau. The walker may

contributed to the development of the area. He too did much to alleviate the hardships endured locally during the bad years of the Famine. It is said that he would often walk to this cairn from his house at Drumnasole on the coast road to sit, read and reflect. The Turnley family were both wealthy, benign and influential. They had a huge influence on the development of the Glens and on the nearby town of Cushendall. Francis Turnley went to work in China in 1796 and is reputed to have returned with a profit of some £80,000 - an immense fortune in those days.

To the north, in the distance, views of Scotland can often be seen on the horizon. To the west stands Trostan, the highest mountain in Antrim at 550 metres and Collin Top slightly further to the south looms large.

The sight of a large expanse of water known as Lough Natullig signifies the end of the most open and exposed area of the Garron Plateau. There is a small stream called the Altmore Burn which runs from it down into Glenariff. Closer to Glenariff, panoramic views open on every side, and it is easy to appreciate, why Glenariff has earned the title of 'Queen of the Glens'. On the far side of the valley the ladder farms that typify farming practices in this Glen can be clearly seen. The upper part of these strips of field are of poor quality, while those at the bottom are rich in soil and highly fertile. A century ago the local farmers worked these steep hillsides with a horse and a 'slide car.' It

Looking down into Glenariff

Glenariff valley with Waterfoot in the distance & Layde headland beyond

consisted of two long poles which slid along the ground on iron runners. The poles were joined together by cross beams which provided a platform that could carry manure, turf, stooks of hay and other loads up and down the sloping ground. The use of the slide car was common throughout the Glens, but it was used in many other areas of rural Ireland as well.

Glenariff is a text book example of a glaciated valley. It is in fact understood to be one of the finest in the British Isles. However the Glens are unusual in the world of Glaciation. Glaciers usually form in high mountains and flow slowly downhill. The Glens were carved by sea ice moving inland from the coast.

The descent down the side of Glenariff can be steep and very wet in sections so care is needed. A narrow gauge track once ran along the top side of the glen in the late 1800's linking the iron ore mines in Glenravel with the coast at Red Bay. The ore was originally taken all the way by horse and cart until in 1872 an overhead wire tramway was constructed which ran as far as the pier at Red Bay and naturally made the shipping of the ore much easier. The ore was loaded into large buckets that bore it down the valley at 'phone line height' to be loaded on board ship. Buckets loaded with ore travelled slowly overhead down one side of the wire tramway. The empty buckets came up on the other side. The load exceeded 200 tons per day. However,

Remains of the old overhead cable

the system was barely in use when it was sabotaged in 1873 by a number of carters who resented losing the business that the transport of ore had hitherto offered. It was never erected again. Its use would in any event have been curtailed by the construction of a narrow gauge railway line that was laid to connect the mines with the coast. A section of it ran for several miles along the banks of the Glenariff River. Little trace remains of this railway now though evidence of it is still there in the form of the levelled ground that bore the sleepers and the pillars which once supported a small viaduct over the river.

At this point, the scenery changes dramatically in that the surrounding landscape is hedged and cultivated. The wide open spaces of the hill give way to the meadowland of the valley floor. The Glenariff River flows through the valley. The course of the river has been altered in order to alleviate hitherto severe flooding problems. All of the rivers in the Glens are prone to flooding due to their steep sides and the short distance between source and sea.

The high sides of Glenariff reach up and away from the river. The only thing not dwarfed by those cliffs in Glenariff is the wind, and there are times when it will propel you headlong down the glen to the conclusion of this walk in the village of Waterfoot.

Cushendall and Glenariff

Glenariff waterfall

This walk departs Cushendall by way of the famous coast road that skirts Red Bay and that leads to Waterfoot village. The Sea of Moyle lies to the left and the broad, generous headlands of Garron and Layde are in front and behind respectively. On the outskirts of the village stands the old coastguard cottage on the edge of the shore, near the Boat Club, and the Life Boat Station. It is appropriate that both are centres of excellence, for there is a long and honourable tradition of seamanship in Cushendall and the Glens. The local lifeboat crew is dedicated, committed and thorough in its unselfish service.

A short distance into the walk the road passes under a well-known landmark known far and wide as the Red Bay arch. Situated above it are the ruins of an ancient castle which at one time was the chief dwelling place of the McDonnells, the Lords of the Isles. It was besieged and burned by Shane O'Neill in 1565 on one of his forays into the locality and was re-built by the McDonnells before they abandoned it in 1597 in order to move North to their new

Red Bay Castle

stronghold at Dunluce. The caves above the arch are believed to have been used by them for the storage of food and weaponry.

This road leading to Waterfoot is part of the route taken by the parade of dignitaries and participants on the opening day of the first Glens' Feis. Feis Na nGleann was and still is a popular event, a celebration of local and national culture. It was the brainchild of the Belfast antiquarian and collector Francis Joseph Biggar who was influential in promoting Gaelic culture throughout the North. There is a famous photograph taken by the well-known Robert J. Welch of the occasion. It shows Biggar leading the procession and in the long line of men and women that day following behind the banner there were local enthusiasts like Miss Margaret Dobbs of Portnagolan House and Miss Ada McNeill of Cushendun, as well as better known luminaries like Roger Casement, Douglas Hyde, (subse-

quently first President of the Irish Republic), the poet Joseph Campbell, (author of My Lagan Love), Sir Horace Plunkett, Ronald McNeill (later Lord Cushendun) and a large number of participants from Rathlin. There were musicians, choirs, marching bands. All the houses along the route were newly whitewashed, and out in the bay lay a small flotilla of gaily decorated yachts. It was a big day in the cultural life of the Glens. The date - Thursday, June 30th, 1904.

Just past the arch you pass the Red Bay harbour and pier, now rarely used commercially. At one time, the pier was used by sailing ships bringing in cargo like building materials, stone, machinery and household coal for the area, as well as for the export of small quantities of local limestone and iron ore. More recently the harbour was the point of departure for a passenger ferry running between Red Bay and Campbelltown.

Just before Waterfoot village there are a small number of caves cut in the sandstone. The larger cave was once the home of a lesser dignitary called Annie Murray. No one seems to know her reasons for choosing to live in a cave, but she lived there from her fiftieth year to the time of her death, by which time she was over a hundred years of age. Annie was a well-known whisky maker. There is a story which suggests that in order to avoid any payment of revenue to the government of the time, she charged for water but not for the liquor. Mr and Mrs Hall who toured Ireland in the 1840's and who kept a journal of their visit to the 'rude' Irish came to her humble shebeen and recorded their encounter with Annie Murray. Their recollection of Annie was not altogether flattering.

"Her swollen person and appearance suggested to us a resemblance to the toads which are found embedded in the sandstone rocks and which thrive without air; from the blackened ceiling of her 'den', the heavy damps distilled in great drops, while the smoke struggled to escape through the door, and the room was reeking with the smell of poteen."

The Halls were not the only 'gentry' to visit. Annie Murray was an object of much curiosity among visitors to the Glens in those days. She had a son and it was said locally that he was murdered by a half wit on the road nearby. She herself died in 1847 and she was buried in the nearby graveyard at Kilmore.

Waterfoot stands at the narrow mouth of the Glenariff River which at one time flooded the houses whenever there was a particularly high tide. The high basalt plateau of Lurigedan mountain dominates the village. On the prow of the mountain there is an impressive example of an early Iron Age promontory fort. It consists of a series of closely related ramparts that follow the contours of the plateau from one side to the other. It must have provided a formi-

Red Bay Arch

dable defense system, for the slopes of Lurigedan are steep and any potential attackers would have thought long and hard before attempting any assault on the people who occupied the ground between the ramparts and the cusp of

Waterfoot village & beach

the mountain. The site is some forty acres in size and that suggests a tribal refuge of local importance, but one that wasn't permanently occupied, given its exposed position. The site has never been properly excavated and probably never will but, at one time it must have featured prominently in the lives of the people living in the immediate vicinity of Red Bay.

Waterfoot is a small village with its back to the shore. The beach at Waterfoot is not attractive in the conventional sense. There are beaches all along this particular coastline that are much easier on the eye, but the Waterfoot shore is

accessible and provides an alternative to the village pavements. The coast road leads on to Carnlough, Glenarm and Larne by way of Garron Point. The road wasn't built until the mid 1830's and until then, the Glens were remote and relatively inaccessible. There was a rough track between Larne and Cushendall, but it climbed and dipped over each rocky headland, and the journey was uncomfortable and even dangerous at times. Thomas Hore, a lieutenant with the Royal Engineers and one of the men involved in the Ordnance Survey of 1833 wrote about sections that were *"tremendously and frightfully steep"* and commented that the journey contained some commanding views of the sea, *"if one could turn his eye from the frightful precipice at his feet."* Richard Dobbs who surveyed the Glens in depth wrote of the necessity of having a guide on the journey from Glenarm to Red Bay, and added that *"the journey was not to be commended either in Summer or in Winter."* Hardly an observation designed to encourage the outsider to come in.

Visitors to the middle Glens in those days were few and only the intrepid and the curious really bothered to explore them. Consequently, the people of the area acquired a reputation for being quite different to their fellow countrymen in the rest of Ireland. Dobbs described them as being,

"distinct in their features, manners and accent....remarkable for their honesty... industrious and very hospitable.....peaceable and well conducted, except that they are very fond of whisky drinking."

He also noted that there were many who had no understanding of the English language, for they could only speak in Gaelic, the language most widely spoken throughout the Glens at that time

The building of the Coast Road had a huge impact on the countryside and local villages. It not only provided easy access for the outsider; it also allowed Glens folk access to the wider world, as well as to their neighbours to the North and South along the coast. The road was built by the Scottish engineer, William Bald who took a radical decision and blasted the high cliffs right down to sea level. The resulting stone and debris provided the foundations which were subsequently smoothed and surfaced to form the modern road.

From Waterfoot this walk now takes you inland away from the coast, into Glenariff Glen probably the best known of the nine Glens and certainly among the most varied and dramatic. The road leads you into the heart of Glenariff with its pattern of small farms in the valley and ladder farms on the slopes. The proximity of the shore played an important role in the lives of the farmers who worked the small fields in places like Glenariff. They used the seaweed that was washed ashore in large quantities, as fertiliser, and they also used it as a kind of cash crop. Each year in the late Spring, it was collected in bundles and piled into stooks along the shore where it soon dried in the Summer wind. It was then taken by cart to a stone kiln, called a kelp kiln, where it was slowly roasted and burned over a fire of whins. The ash that accumulated was allowed to cool and to harden. It was then bro-

Heading into Glenariff in the rain

Barn Door

ken into lumps and exported to be used in the manufacture of iodine and silver iodide in the expanding photographic business.

In wet weather several waterfalls tumble and spill dramatically for hundreds of feet down the steep sides of Glenariff. In times of flood, they provide one of the most dramatic sights in the whole area. The series of smaller waterfalls further up the valley has considerably enhanced the beauty of this wonderful glen. It was the reputation they enjoyed that attracted tourists to Glenariff for decades and they are well worth a visit at any time of the year, but particularly in the Spring and the early Summer when the wild flowers are in bloom, and the air is scented with the sweet aroma of the wild garlic that grows in profusion along the river banks and in every shaded hollow. The road leads to a well-known hostelry that was once a tea house called Laragh Lodge. The entrance to the wooded glen is right beside it and the pathway is narrow and steep betimes. It follows the course of the river and leads to the two best known water-

Wild Garlic

falls. Ess-na Laragh and the very dramatic Ess-na Craoibhe. The pathways of Glenariff were laid out by the old Belfast and Northern Counties Railway Company. The English novelist William Thackeray, who travelled extensively in Ireland, arrived at Glenariff as part of the 'grand tour' he made, by way of preparation for his Irish Sketch Book, published in the early 1870's. Thackeray was extravagant in his praise, and referred to the glen as being like a miniature Switzerland *"joining together cataracts, valleys, rushing streams and blue mountains."* Effusive but well deserved comment from the great man. His observations were endorsed in 1902 by another English writer, Stephen Gwynne who encouraged the visitor to visit the waterfalls in wet weather;

"If by any chance it should be a day of pelting rain, why then go all the more. These mountain streams fill with extra-ordinary rapidity and a finer sight no one need wish for."

In the early years of the last century tourists and day trippers travelled to Glenariff by way of the old Northern Railways narrow gauge line that took them to Parkmore Station, at the very top of the glen where it intersects with Glenballyemon. They then travelled by horse drawn vehicle to where the falls commenced, and from there they followed the winding pathway that followed the river and which crossed and recrossed its rapid descent. They could either rejoin their transport at the tea house at Laragh Lodge for the return to Parkmore Station, or they could alternatively continue along the Coast Road to Larne, and from there take another train to Belfast. The increasing popularity of the motor car and the subsequent decline of the railway system gradually led to the demise of the Parkmore line in 1930 and the formal excursion trip to the waterfalls ceased to be a regular feature of tourism in Glenariff.

The road leading back out of 'Laragh Lodge' forks to the left and leads to the main Ballymena-Cushendall road affording excellent views of the

The tumbling river in Glenariff

The wooden bridge at Ess-na Craoibhe

ed grove and it was at one time much larger. The road actually cuts through what was once a part of the burial ground. The old church, which was built from wood has gone entirely but Rev. O'Laverty one of the main authorities on the history of the area and author of the well-known history of the Diocese of Down and Connor is of the opinion that Kilmore was once an important ecclesiastical site.

Glenariff is still relatively well populated and it is reckoned to have been one of the sites visited regularly by early visitors to the North Antrim coast. A skeleton which was discovered on a Glenariff farm in 1946 was that of an Early Bronze Age man. The skeleton was discovered in a cist lined with stone slabs. Beside it was a small decorated urn that at one time probably held food of some kind

Kilmore Graveyard

glen below as it sweeps majestically towards the sea and Red Bay. This can be a busy thoroughfare during the tourist season, so walk cautiously, and preferably in single file. The route leads past an ancient graveyard on the left called Kilmore. It is situated above the road in a small shad-

to provide sustenance during the journey to the other world. Several similar graves have been discovered in North Antrim, and there was a theory held by a Professor Walmsley, who was attached to the Anatomy Department of Queens University at the time, that these were the remains of a man whose ancestors had left Persia around 1500 BC. They had then

The Heart of Glenariff

made their way along the Danube and across Europe. Some of them had ventured on towards Scotland and a few had crossed over to Ulster. This early ancestor had presumably remained and had been buried in Glenariff.

The road skirts the high cliffs of Lurigedan and its cascading waterfalls. In wet weather they are dramatic while in dry weather they are reduced to a trickle, but the views ahead and on either side will more than compensate for any feelings of disappointment, should you have any, on your return to the Coast Road and Cushendall.

Cushendall and Cushendun

These two villages have been synonymous with life in the middle Glens for generations and today they are still central to the social, cultural and commercial activity of the area. They are frequently mentioned in the same breath, like Romulus and Remus, but each place has its own distinctive atmosphere, and despite their close proximity they are quite different and separate. In fact they are traditional rivals, each village protective of its own identity, and that rivalry is best instanced and observed each time they meet on the hurling field, where the competition is intense. There are however few walks in the Glens guaranteed to please as much as the walk that brings you to Cushendun by way of Layde, and back again to Cushendall. It is a walk of some ten miles, but it can be shortened, and it is far from strenuous.

The Cliff Path

The shore at Cushendall

which begins at the far end of the beach. Cushendall Golf Club has one of the most charming courses in Ireland, and one of the most interesting crests. It consists of crossed golf clubs and four swans, a tribute to those sad and lovely Children of Lir, turned into white swans and banished by their evil godmother Aoife to swim the restless Sea of Moyle for seven hundred long bitter years. The legendary fate that befell Fionnuala, Aed, Fiacra and Conn is fittingly symbolised by that crest.

The early stages are inauspicious enough if you begin, as I suggest you do, in the car park beside the Cushendall Boat Club on the road to Waterfoot. It is but a short walk through the nearby caravan park to reach the true beginning of the walk. The Sea of Moyle lies on the right; the Mull of Kintyre dominates the far horizon, assuming of course you can see the horizon, for the visibility is as fickle as the weather. The braes of Layde lie ahead. Following the rocky shoreline the route brings you past a small headland and down to the Dall River from which Cushendall derives its name, Cóis an Dall - the foot of the Dall. Crossing the bridge you pass by the golf club and head for the cliff path

The cliff path is narrow, rutted and uneven. It rises up and away from the shore. The climb is steep initially but well worth the effort. There are few cliff paths to equal this one with its superb views of sea, shore and mountain. Behind and below lies the beach; beyond the beach lies Cushendall and beyond again, the long slopes of Lurigedan, the mountain that separates Glenariff and Glenballyemon. The Salmon Port where the fishing catches were landed can be seen far below and as the path rises the panorama becomes more dramatic. On a fine day it has few equals. The path skirts behind the gardens of some houses, including the substantial sandstone residence, Portnagolan, that once was the home of Miss Margaret Dobbs, an ascendancy woman who had a zeal for all things Irish, including the language. She was a minor playwright, an acquaintance of the then Poet Laureate, John Masefield, and a close friend of Roger Casement who was a regular visitor to Portnagolan.

The cliff path leads to Layde Churchyard, but if you so choose you can take the narrow track on the right which will bring you down to the shore at Port Obb (though anyone who descends to the shore should be prepared for a steep climb back to Layde). Don't expect to find anything resembling a conventional port although, there was a small harbour of some description there centuries ago. Obb is an old Norse word for port, and at one time it was a traditional belief that this was the place St. Patrick came to during his flight from Slemish and that he found a ship which took him to safety.

Layde Graveyard

The graveyard at Layde is one of the oldest in the Glens. The original church is mentioned in the 'Taxation of Pope Nicholas IV' in 1288. The small church that stands there today was built in the late seventeenth century and although it is widely referred to as a Franciscan Friary, it was in fact a parish church. Local legend relates

Dr James DrDonnells gravestone

that it at one time had a strong connection with St. Kieran, who is reputed to have founded a small community there.

Layde graveyard contains a large number of old graves with headstones. Some have been damaged by the weather; a small number have been vandalised, but a remarkable number are in good condition. One of the more impressive contains the remains of Dr James McDonnell, 'The father of Belfast medicine', co-organiser of the famous Harp Festival of 1792, held in the Exchange Rooms, Belfast, and a man well acquainted with people like Wolfe Tone, Henry Joy McCracken, Thomas Russell and other radicals of his time.

One of the most mysterious headstones stands beside the stile entrance. It consists of an upright sandstone pillar with a round hole in the centre and it is believed to have been brought over from Scotland by the first McDonnells who settled in the area. It resembles other stones of pagan origin found throughout Ulster, particularly in the Glencolum-

bkille district of South Donegal. The headstone is known as Cross Na Naghan. The local Glens of Antrim Historical Society have published a small book containing a unique and thorough record of the various old graves in Layde.

The name Layde is believed by some to be a derivation of the Christian name Lydia, and there is a legend that tells how she fled from Scotland, being betrothed to a man she didn't love. She sought refuge at Layde and subsequently on Knocklayde Mountain near Ballycastle where she was captured and killed by her pursuers.

The laneway leading out of the Churchyard connects with the road that will bring you up and over Layde mountain. If the weather is benign and the sky clear, the walker is guaranteed dramatic views of the seascape and the hills. The road leads you past Layde House, a sturdy, substantial building on the right. It was at one time the residence of Hugh Flatley who came

Cross Na Naghan

from Mayo to teach in Glenaan School and who took Irish classes locally.

Just beyond Layde house there is a small cottage and beside it the ruins of an old castle. The house is empty now, but at one time it was a local Mecca for any one with a yarn to tell or a song to sing. The eminent folklorist Michael J. Murphy came to live in it during the early fifties when he was dispatched by the Irish Folk Lore Commission to compile and record what remained in the locality of traditional lore, custom and story.

The director and founder of the Commission in Dublin was a renowned scholar, Professor James Hamilton Delargy, a man with strong Glens connections. Murphy recorded whatever he could throughout the Glens. Most of it had to do with fairy faith and local legend. He managed to preserve much of what remained; stories about the legendary Finn McCool, fragments about the Glens fairy man called the gruagach, and lore about cures for various ailments. Michael J. was an experienced and knowledgeable collector, but even back in the fifties whatever remained was dying fast. Today, despite widespread belief to the contrary, practically nothing remains of an oral tradition that was rich, unique and varied. Professor Hamilton Delargey has also been forgotten, despite the fact that he was responsible for the foundation of a Folklore institute that is among the finest in Europe.

Despite his rural background and his affinity with local folk lore: despite his vast knowledge of life in the Glens in bygone years, and irrespective of the fact that he had come to live in the locality, Murphy was still seen as a 'runner'- an outsider. In the Glens of Antrim you are a 'runner' until you have at least two centuries of Glens blood coursing in your veins. Ironically, many of those who choose to use the term disparagingly would themselves fail to qualify as being of true Glens origin. It seems that many would like to be called, but few are chosen.

The Layde road continues to climb for at least another mile, but the rise is steady and the quality of the view is undiminished. On a really clear day you can see with the naked eye the white outline of the lighthouse on the Mull of Kintyre and with binoculars you should be able to see the small village of Macrahanish to the right of it. The mouth of Campbelltown Loch is visible, as is the Firth of Clyde. The local historian and founder member of the Glens of Antrim Historical Society, Jack McCann used to remark that if you looked at the history of Ireland with your back to Scotland, you were looking at Ireland with *"one eye shut"*. You cannot walk this road and not be reminded of the truth of that remark. The fields slope sharply downwards towards the rocky shore. Local farmers frequently unearthed a variety of Neolithic implements when ploughing. Many of those artifacts are now in the Ulster Museum in Belfast. A less charming and more obvious symbol of modern life greets you on the landward side at the crest of the hill. A communications mast stands like a steel sentry, dominating an hitherto delightful skyline. It marks the beginning of the descent into Knocknacarry village.

The most remarkable thing about Knocknacarry is the rate at which it is developing. It is also one of the few places of similar size in Ireland that has no pub. There was a well-known hostelry in Knocknacarry some time ago. Pat Hamiltons Bar was a venue greatly favoured by a clientele who came from near and far at weekends.

Just a short walk from Knocknacarry brings you to Cushendun. A whole variety of adjectives have been employed down the years to describe Cushendun, all of them quite appropriate - picturesque, charming, quaint, delightful, pretty. Each of them is applicable, for Cushendun is uniquely situated, and the rows of Cornish style cottages give it a slightly surreal atmosphere, as if the village lay between two worlds. That is in many ways apt for the square and the Cornish style cottages were designed by the architect Clough William Ellis who also designed the Welsh village of

The river & the bridge at Glendun

Portmeirion, used as the location for a well-known fantasy series on television starring Patrick McGoohan, called 'The Prisoner'.

At one time there were three hotels adjoining the harbour, an indication of Cushendun's popularity with visitors from Ireland and Scotland. The Cushendun Hotel will be remembered by many as the location of 'The Blue Room', a small back bar in the hotel that became a venue for folk singers and musicians from all over the North. There is little music to be heard in Cushendun today. The only public house in Cushendun is well-known, and McBrides Bar is the property of the National Trust, as is all of the village and shore.

All that remains of Castle Carra

The long white house at the far end of the beach is known as Rockport and it was the dwelling place of Lady Cushendun, better known as the poet Moira O'Neill, author of 'Songs of the Glens of Antrim' and mother of another well-known writer, Molly Keane. The house was subsequently lived in by the celebrated painter James Humbert Craig. To the rear stand all that remains of Castle Carra where Shane O'Neill, warlike Prince of Ulster, 'Shane the Proud,' is sup-

posed to have met his untimely death under the knife blades of his mortal enemies the McDonnells. The Castle was probably built in the 13th or 14th century and it was one of the many small castles, built by lesser lords and common throughout Ireland and Scotland. Castle Carra was probably built by the Byssets or the Mc Flynns, two families of power and influence at the time.

At this point the road divides. The right hand fork leads to Ballycastle by way of Tor, one of the most scenic roads in

The middle road

Ireland. Our route now turns left and follows the winding road that in a short time leads to another junction. Left once more, cross the River Dun and you soon arrive back in Knocknacarry. The main road that runs between Cushendun and Cushendall can be busy in the Summer months and demands caution. After approximately half a mile the main road swings to the right, but a narrower road leads straight ahead. It is known locally as 'the middle road', and it leads you straight back into Cushendall by way of the townland of Coshkib.

This is a road of much charm. It rises gradually and affords wonderful views of the middle Glens area. Glencorp lies below and Gruaig Mountain stands on the right. In the far distance the unmistakable outline of Tievebulliagh juts out of the hills that rise to meet the broad slopes of Trostan, and after a mile or two you are looking down into the small fields and farms of Glenaan. It was in Coshkib that one of the most famous houses in the Glens stood. It was a renowned 'ceile house': a place for music, song and small talk. It was the home of the Hyndman family and when the last occupant died - the renowned Dan Hyndman - the house was taken down stone by stone and rebuilt at the Ulster Folk and Transport Museum in Cultra. Today it is known as the Cushendall Farmhouse.

Looking across at Tievebulliagh

The narrow road dips and rises slightly, but shortly before you reach the outskirts of Cushendall you pass the cone shaped hill on the left known as Tieveragh. A volcanic plug, it was once associated with fairy lore and widely believed by local children to be the home of an entire colony of the 'little people.' Many of the stories and yarns recorded locally in the nineteen fifties by the distinguished author and BBC radio producer Sam Hanna Bell, had to do with the fairies on Tieveragh and their mischievous forays into the nearby Glens. Up until the early years of the last century some old people still believed the stories about the 'changelings,' infants who were stolen from the cradle by the fairies and a fairy child put there in its place. Belief in the banshee was also widespread, the fairy woman who was the messenger of death. She could be heard at night wailing and crying outside in the dark. The banshee was said to follow certain families, and some people would swear they had seen her, perched on a rooftop or on the side of a ditch.

Beyond Tieveragh you once again catch sight of the sea and the rooftops of Cushendall as you commence your descent into the village by way of High Street. The steep incline brings you down past the headquarters of the Ardclinis Activity Centre. A large town house that once housed the local hospital, it is now one of the finest privately run outdoor centres in Northern Ireland. The centre offers a variety of courses and offers wet suits and cycles for hire. It plays an important role in promoting the village and the locality both at home and abroad.

The old hospital was founded in 1885 by Nurse Katherine Ann Stewart McDonnell, one of a family of ten. Their father John was an esteemed doctor, Medical Poor Law Commissioner for Ireland and obviously someone highly regarded within the

The old hospital now Ardclinis Activity Centre

profession. Her grandfather was someone equally renowned Dr James McDonnell, referred to previously as founder of the Belfast Medical School, which subsequently developed into the Royal Victoria Hospital. The quality of the nursing care in the Cushendall Cottage Hospital was frequently praised over the years, even after it had moved to its new site on the road to the shore. Regrettably, there is no longer a hospital in the Glens.

The centre of the village is dominated by the curfew tower, also known as Turnleys Tower. It was built in 1821 and was reputedly designed to resemble the kind of tower Turnley saw during his travels in China. The stone used in the construction was probably drawn from the nearby Red Bay and the first custodian of the tower was one Dan McBride traditionally believed to have been a soldier in Wellington's army at Waterloo. The tower acted as a local jail - there was a small dungeon in the basement - and the bell was rung throughout the day at eight in the morning and again at one o'clock at six and at nine o'clock in the evening. In return for this service, the tenant occupied the tower free of rent. Today the building serves as a small residential arts centre for writers and painters.

Cushendall Pub

The centre of Cushendall has changed but little over the years. It still retains much of its traditional charm. Queen Elizabeth made a 'grant' of it in 1574 to Henry Knollys, Comptroller of her Household. She referred to it as Bournay Dall. The Hollow Blade Company of London owned it for a while and then it passed into the control of yet another English resident, a Dr Richardson who changed the name to Newtown Glens. Francis Turnley purchased it and restored its name to an approximation of the old Gaelic name Cóis an Dall (foot of the Dall river). It contains three fine public houses, a variety of eating houses and a hotel. In any of these you can obtain some well earned refreshment before completing your walk.

The old farmhouse at Savagh

The walk through these two adjoining middle Glens is a pleasure at any time of the year. It brings you past fields and small farms; past moorland and mountain and along the banks of several small fast flowing rivers and streams. You may choose to walk these Glens in any order, but I suggest that you ascend Glenaan and then descend Glendun, for Glendun is considerably longer than Glenaan and so the overall walk will be less strenuous but nonetheless pleasant. You should use two cars if possible; one to bring you to the start of the walk, and the other to bring you back to where you started. The walk should end at the Church in lower Glendun.

I suggest you begin at the foot of Glenaan. You will pass Glenaan Primary School, built in 1899, situated on the banks of the Glenaan River and facing towards Glencorp. The pupils have planted a small wild flower garden that decorates the roadside. Most of them come from Cushendall and only a few are from the glen, for Glenaan, like so many of the Antrim Glens is underpopulated. My father was a pupil at Glenaan School and he was reared in the immediate townland of Lubitavish. In his time there were over fifty children from the locality attending the school. Today most of the pupils come from Cushendall.

Glenaan School

As you walk the Glens you will pass the ruins of houses once occupied, along the road and on the brae face. Some of those families moved to Cushendall: others headed for Glasgow: the more adventurous emigrated to America in search of work and a better life. The reality of this is probably best instanced by the ruins of Knockban, a cluster of houses, (known traditionally as a 'clachan'), once occupied and now totally derelict that can still be seen on the hillside above Glenaan. You will probably have to strain your eyes

Farm at Lubitavish

emigrant to say goodbye. The unspoken understanding in bygone days was that those young men and women would not return again. The American Wakes were often more solemn than a wake for the dead.

The emigrants frequently came from different families. They travelled in 'convoys'; in small groups where they could mind one another and share familiar company before parting on the streets of Pittsburg, Chicago or New York. A man living out on Torr Head had an uncle who claimed to have heard the wailing and crying of emigrants on board the schooners that sailed close by on their way to America. They found work in the factories, on the railways and in the steel mills. Many of the girls went to become maids and servants, 'kitchen canaries.' Their descendants are there to this day.

to find Knockban, but scan the hillside to the right and almost opposite to the school and with patience you will detect it.

The 'American Wake' was a regular feature of life in places like Glenaan. These were occasions when friends, neighbours and relations gathered in the house of an intending

A visit to the graveyard in the Green Point district of New York is mute but eloquent testimony to the final resting

Ruins of the Glenaan Mill

You will see several farms in lower Glenaan. Most of them were once self-sufficient, growing flax, corn, potatoes and vegetables. Nowadays the local farms are used to rear sheep and cattle. The ruins of a flax mill on the side of the road in Glenaan is all that remains of a building that was once an important resource for local farmers. Up until the fifties every farm would have its fields of flax and in Summer the air was rank with the heavy smell of the crop retting in the small flax dams or 'dubs.' The mill was one of several in the area, and this particular one was in operation back in 1834

place of men and women with Glens names like McAuley, McKeegan, McAllister, McCambridge, McDonnell, Darragh and McKay.

The Glens were not as sorely affected by the Great Famine as other areas of Ireland and there is nothing to indicate enforced evictions. Poverty, hardship, the want of a better life were the key factors behind emigration from the Glens. Many of those who emigrated in the 1920s found themselves in even greater difficulties when they were so badly hit by the Depression, that hard earned money had to be sent out to America to bring them home again to the small farms they thought they had left behind.

Looking back at Tiveragh Hill

when it may have been a corn mill. The corn mills were in production up until the mid 19th century. Their decline reflected the growth of the road and rail systems, whereby flour and meal were brought in from the big towns. This particular mill regularly had problems with the flow of water in the Glenaan River, and a tractor had to be sometimes used to provide power for the machinery.

About half a mile beyond the site of the old mill you will come to a laneway on the left which will lead you to 'Ossians Grave.' Cross the small bridge over the Glenaan River and keep going straight ahead. The lane is very steep and the 'grave' is situated in a field about a mile away, so this diversion must not be made lightly. The visit to Ossian's Grave will take time and effort. The grave is in fact a Neolithic court cairn that commands an impressive view of the countryside. There is nothing impressive however about this ancient monument, not even to the eye of the most enthusiastic early historian. The stones are narrow and set in a rough circle with a smaller circle at the Western segment, and its association with the legendary Ossian, bard to Finn McCool stems from a local tradition that he was born and reared on Lurigedan Mountain.

Ossian is reputed to have fallen in love with a woman from the Underworld and he went there to live and be with her. After a period of apparent nuptial bliss, he decided to make a visit to the world he had left behind. Ossian was

Ossians Grave

warned before he began the journey, not to place a foot on the ground of Glenaan. He went on horseback, and everything was fine until he bent in the saddle to help an old woman. His saddle slipped, and the once proud and handsome Ossian fell to the ground and turned to dust.

James Boyle who was a civil assistant on the Ordnance Survey Memoir for the Parish of Layd in 1835 noted how he had *"spent much time in listening to the innumerable legends, stories and traditions which are recited in the more remote parts of this parish. They mostly refer to nothing but the fabled deeds of Fin Mac Coul and the many other giants and enchanters who made Glenariff and Lurgedon Hill the scene of their exploits. They are inconsistent, contradictory and absurd: enchantment forms the leading feature in all their legends, and there is not one of them which throws any light or tends to corroborate any incident in history or record"*.

Whatever his qualities as a chronicler and observer, James Boyle was obviously not of a lyrical disposition. His comments are those of a government official and I doubt if he would have impressed the Ulster poet John Hewitt who loved this immediate area, and who praised both place and people in his wonderful collection of poems 'The Day of the Corncrake,' illustrated lavishly with paintings by my uncle, the late Charles McAuley who spent his infancy in the townland of Lubitavish where Ossians Grave stands. Nearby, at the gateway to the field stands John Hewitt's

memorial cairn, a simple but fitting symbol of remembrance to the poet who lived in the Glens for several years.

John Hewitt Memorial Cairn

I stop to name the peaks along their dark array
For these are more than mountains, shouldered clear
into the sharp star- pointed atmosphere,
into then sunset. They mark out and bound
the utmost limits of my chosen ground.....”

Hewitt commemorated and celebrated a dying way of life in that collection, a book of poetry that accurately evokes the atmosphere of the middle Glens fifty years ago. The cairn was erected by the members of the esteemed John Hewitt Summer School.

In Summer and Autumn the Glenaan road is lined with fuschia and honeysuckle. Whatever the season it is a pleasant walk. The surrounding hills protect the lower glen. To the left the broad flank of Tievebulliagh mountain rises up and away from the river down below. On the right the glen is guarded by sloping hills, stone walled and heather covered with ancient names like names like Falmacrilly, Tavnaghoney, Eshery and Tavnaghdrissagh. The higher slopes are dotted with the sparse bent outlines of hawthorn bushes. Locally they are known as skeaghs and their presence is partly attributable to the fact that no one dare cut them down, not even when they are growing in arable land. The tradition of the ‘fairy thorn’ exists all over Ireland. It was there in Druidic times and the Glens are still full of stories concerning misfortunate people who tried to do damage to the skeaghs, like the man who intended to cut

Red Fuschia, Green Gate

one down and who broke his leg in a fall the night before, or the farmer with similar intentions whose house and byre burned to the ground.

The walk to the top of the glen is some three miles long. There is still evidence of a way of life that is fast disappearing. There are new houses and bungalows where once there were thatched cottages. There are turf banks no longer in use, and the forage harvesters lumber up and down the narrow road, but in Spring and Summer the sheep and lambs still graze and the larks sing high above the mountain. The

Moorland at the head of Glenaan

miles and you are now at the head of Glendun. The walk is now more or less downhill all the way.

The fast flowing Dun River is below on the right. It has a short journey to the sea and at one time it was prized by anglers as a fine salmon river. In recent years catches of salmon and trout have been poor. The Dun floods easily and rapidly. There was a sudden flood in the early Autumn of 1990 probably as a result of a cloudburst on the top of Glendun. A wall of water built rapidly and surged down the glen at great speed washing rocks, stones, trees, bushes and livestock into the sea far below. It happened at night and fortunately no one was injured. In November 1963, a landslide carried tons of wet earth and mud into the river. So great was the mass of debris that the course of the river was permanently changed.

views from the head of the glen are spectacular. Behind, you can see the run of the coast as far as Garron Point with Scotland in the distance. Below on the right lies Glendun and a little further along the road you can see the long sweep of hillside that runs to meet the slopes of Trostan Mountain. Descend the hill, cross the river and turn right at the signpost. At this point you will have completed four

James Boyle in his survey of 1835 had noted that the river *'owing to the height of its numerous sources and tributary streams is very subject to sudden and rapid floods which prove very destructive to the country through which it passes, frequently stripping the fields of their soil and vegetation and covering them with quantities of stones'*

Moments of drama however are scarce in the glen. Like neighbouring Glenaan, its population has been greatly depleted, and once again the evidence is there in the ruined houses and in the once worked fields with their lazy beds. You can see the outline of the beds on the slopes on the far side of the road. The soil at this elevation is thin and lazy beds provided an extra layer of soil for the growing of potatoes, barley and oats. A strip of ground about the length of a spade was marked out and manure spread along it. The sods on either side were folded over on top of the strip. The crop was then planted into the sods by means of a dibbler. The resulting harvest was used to feed the family. In a bad year the people went hungry. So much for the romance of 'the good old days,' but there can be no doubting the fact that Glendun was once home to a thriving and tightly bonded community of hill farmers.

Glendun River

Further down the glen a narrow metal footbridge spans the river. This is the townland of Savagh and this is where my grandfather Bernard McAuley was born and reared. My grandmother Elizabeth McElheron was reared on the other side of the road in the place known as Drumfaskey. Their trysting was a well kept secret, for theirs was a 'mixed marriage' between a Catholic and a Protestant, something not

The river below Savagh

Beside the footbridge you can see a ruined tree. At one time it was a majestic sight, with a thick trunk and spreading branches. It was known as 'The Tailors Bush' named after a journeyman tailor who travelled the Glens making clothes to order. He frequently plied his trade in the shade of the tree. My great grandfather remembered him working there. However, a more chilling tradition says that a man called Taylor who worked for the Crommelin family hanged himself on the tree, and that thereafter the tree got the reputation of being the site of regular hauntings. 'The Tailors Bush' was badly damaged by the great flood of 1963, when that giant wall of water swept down the river taking the old bridge along with it. The roots of the tree were laid bare and it never recovered.

lightly entered into. 'Mixed marriages' were not approved of in those days, so in true romantic fashion they eloped on horseback one night and were married the next day in Glenarm.

Glendun means 'the brown glen' and the name accurately describes the fast flowing river that runs more or less parallel to the road. Until a few years ago it enjoyed a reputation among fishermen for the quality of its trout and salmon. That is no longer the case for stocks have been sorely depleted and the Dun will take a long time to recover from pollution, poaching and over fishing. Further downstream you will pass the John McSparran memorial farm, situated on the far side of the river. It was donated to the Ulster Wildlife Trust who aim to run it as a traditional farm, with an accompanying tree nursery for indigenous timber. The farm can be accessed by a laneway leading to a ford on the river, (not a practical proposition when the water is high), or by a laneway a few hundreds of yards distant.

The road will lead you to the viaduct, otherwise known as the Big Bridge. It spans both sides of the glen and it took five years to build, (1834 - 1839) for no work was done on it during the winter months. The architect was Charles Lanyon whose name is closely associated with the design of Queens University, as well as some of the magnificent station facades that used to adorn the Ulster Railway. The stone was quarried in Layde, brought by boat to Cushendun and then by horse drawn cart to the site. The bridge was built with local labour. The average wage was just under a shilling a day and many a family in the surrounding Glens was glad to have the income. The government, aware of the military importance of having rapid communications available in the area, was in turn glad to have the road between Cushendall and Ballycastle spanned at this point.

Lanyon's Viaduct

You have now reached the foot of Glendun. Soon you will arrive at a small crossroads and the leafy shade of Craigagh Wood, one of the finest stands of deciduous timber in Northern Ireland and certainly one of the most atmospheric. There is a fine example of a souterrain situated quite close to the gate that leads to the wood. Beyond

Craigagh, on the brow of the hill you will see the outline of the small church where your walk could end. If however you are still in walk mode and mood, you could extend it by another mile and make your way into the village of Knocknacarry. Whatever the decision, a brief visit to the graveyard at St Patricks is worthwhile. An old graveyard and one steeped in local lore, it contains several interesting headstones, but the 'fuldiew' stone is the most memorable.

It lies flat on the ground to the right as you enter and it contains the remains of Charles McAlaster and his son John. The inscription reads,

Early Summer in Glendun

Charles Mc Alaster's burring place.
Here lies the boddy of John his son died 11th
March 1803 Aged 18 years.
Your ship love is mored head and starn for a fuldiew.

Father and son were part of a long and honourable seafaring tradition in the Glens. John was homeward bound when he fell to his death from the ship's rigging. He was to have been paid off at Cushendun where he would have received his 'full due' - hence the name given to the headstone. The local tradition says that his sweetheart spent long hours alone in the graveyard at Craigagh, where she carved the inscription on the stone. Soon afterwards, she was found lying dead on top of his grave.

The mystery that surrounded the word 'fuldiew' was apparently solved by the eminent song collector and antiquarian, Sam Henry who collected widely through the Glens and who was a regular visitor to the places you have just visited on this long but enjoyable walk through Glenaan and Glendun.

Cushendall and Newtown-Crommelin

Looking down towards Glenravel

This cycle begins in the village car park in Cushendall. Cycle to the bridge, over the river Dall, at the end of the car park and turn to the right. Take the next road on the right, signposted Ballymena. It leads directly away from the village and up Glenballyemon. The climb, at first, is gentle, sheltered on one side by the hedgerows and steep banks. The views directly up the glen are dominated by the high slopes of Lurigedan. The fact that this was once a promontory fort explains some of the unusual scars on the mountainside. They are the remains of defensive fortifications.

Lurigedan Mountain

As the road gains h e i g h t, the dark peak of Tievebulliagh is visible to the right, with the bulk of Trostan ahead.

The sharp peaked outline of Tievebulliagh is instantly recognizable and at one time it was a mountain of significance and a place of importance to people of Neolithic times. A large section of the face of Tievebulliagh consists of Porcellanite which was used in the making of early stone implements and weapons such as axes.

The road clings to the steep sides of Lurigedan and marks a clear division between the slopes that are used for grazing and the pasture land lower down the glen. The Ballyemon river has a tendency to flash flood and in October 1990, the river did exactly that, after a prolonged period of very heavy rain. The flood was so swift and high that the river actually burst it's banks, flooded the main street in Cushendall and caused severe damage.

On the opposite side of the glen there is a large crater which serves as the local dump. Its presence is frequently signalled by a rising pall of dark smoke. It is a repository for rubble, household waste, discarded television sets, unwanted prams and bulging bags of black polythene. In fact the black polythene bag is a decorative feature along the hedgerows on that side of Glenballyemon. They can be seen flapping and fluttering like tattered flags of mourning throughout the year. The prominence afforded the dump - prime location, full frontal view, on the side of a glen that is undoubtedly a place of outstanding natural beauty is a continuing source of bewilderment to locals, tourists and passers by.

The road up Glenballyemon

Eventually the climb begins to level out, close to the place known as Retreat. This was once the end of the railway line leading to Ballymena. Retreat was chosen as the end of the line because the steep sides of the Glen made it impossible for the engineers to go much further. There were several branch lines leading off to the mines which at one time were a significant industry in the area – to Dungonnell, Cargan and then to operations with names like Herds Drift and Salmon Drift. The embankment which carried the permanent way runs alongside the road until it disappears among the trees of Parkmore forest.

Further evidence of the railway system can be found at the intersection between the Glenballyemon and Glenariff roads. A large stand of bushes grows beside the road. This was the site of the Parkmore Station which was built in 1888. At that time Glenariff was already a well-known tourist attraction, and the station was built in order to accommodate the rapidly growing tourist traffic. Tourists would arrive at the terminal and then brought the rest of the way by jaunting car. The few buildings which remain do not belong to the original structure which was destroyed in 1921. Parkmore was used as a passenger terminal until 1930, and subsequently as a youth hostel, before it was abandoned.

Close by the station, the marks of the sleepers can still be seen in the ground and the metal water tower is still in place. It was an essential part of the operation at the station, since it was necessary to refill the engine with water, prior to it's return to Ballymena.

The road goes on from here to the village of Cargan, and runs more or less parallel with the railway line. On the hillside there is evidence of the mining industry. Large red scars of clay can be seen, the results of open cast mining, as well as the slag heaps from the more traditional type of underground mine. The iron ore mines provided work for a considerable number of local people, many of whom

Outbuilding at Parkmore

Railway Bridge near Parkmore

would have lived in the village of Cargan and nearby New-town-Crommelin.

In 1870 seven hundred men were employed in these mines. When the Belfast Naturalists Field Club visited the area in 1875 they noted that *"The mountain slopes from Glenravel to Red Bay, formerly seldom visited except by sportsmen, are now burrowed with mines and alive with busy groups of industrious workmen: trains waggons and machinery are active on every side.......the beauty of the scenery has been invaded by the greasy fitters and an army of red stained miners, and the romance of the Glens has been well and truly annihilated."*

Nowadays, Cargan, along with many local villages, is enjoying a regrowth, primarily as dormitory towns for Ballymena and in some cases for Belfast.

Cargan was the site of a distillery, owned by local land owners, Edward and George Benn. The numerous rivers in the area provided the water and the mountain bog provided the peat used to fuel the distillation process, but the venture subsequently collapsed. The Benns were distilling spirit from potatoes, and the authorities decided that this was illegal. Edward Benn appealed the decision arguing that he had brought work to a *"wretched population"* and that he had succeeded in spite of *"stubborn soil and ignorant people."*

They had a substantial house nearby where Edward wrote his renowned History of Belfast, published in 1877. He was also a collector of antiquities, and his collection helped found the original Belfast Museum. George acquired a reputation as a benefactor and an 'improver' and the Benn brothers founded several hospitals in Belfast. It seems that their charity was not manifested in the Glens where they had a reputation for ruthless and mean behaviour in regard to their employees and tenants.

On the 26th of July 1858 while George was standing in his wide bedroom window, a bullet narrowly missed him. It was probably intended for Edward. A £100 reward was promptly offered for the name or cap-

A deserted cottage near Newtown-Crommelin

ture of the perpetrator, but he was never caught. The Benn brothers both survived into old age, and they are buried in Belfast. Edward's ghost is reputed to walk the grounds of his old home in Glenravel.

The road leading through Cargan and on to Ballymena is relatively level, but soon there is a main junction on the

right, signposted 'Orra via Scenic Route' and the climb begins again along this narrow road. It crosses a bridge over the Skerry River and shortly after, it bears to the right, into the village of Newtown-Crommelin.

The village gets it's name from it's founder Nicholas Crommelin. He was a Hugenot, a descendant of the De

– 65 –

throughout the province, and Nicholas inherited a fortune in addition to the name Crommelin. He purchased land in the vicinity in 1800 and set about developing a 'model' village in 1824. His plan centred on his conviction that rough pasture and high mountain could be transformed into agriculturally viable land, using modern ideas, the proper implements and a significant input of his inherited wealth. He spent thousands of pounds on road building schemes, on housing, on building two schools, corn stores and a mill powered by the local river, The Skerry Water. People came from far and wide attracted by the idea of low cost housing and guaranteed employment. Initially everything seemed to be progressing, fuelled by talk of a fine harbour at Cushendun, trade with Ballymena and other places inland, but the schemes never materialised.

Things went from bad to worse and a report in 1832 conjectured that the tenants were not all united in terms of industry, commitment and social standing. Many were simply opportunists, others were not prepared to improve the holdings they were given, and moved on. Those who wanted to see the scheme succeed were gradually disillusioned by the surrounding apathy and the grinding poverty that was insurmountable. The reliance of the settlement on Nicholas Crommelin, and its inability to become self sufficient is made reference to in the Statistical Account of Lieutenant J. Greatorex in September of 1833, for the Ordnance Survey. He notes; *"At present, I believe, Mr Crom-*

A Fairy Thorn

LaCherois family who fled from persecution in their native France in the late 17th century. The De LaCherois were hugely influential in the development of the linen industry

melin receives no rent from the greater portion of the tenants in his parish, as he is anxious to encourage settlers in every way. Even with this liberality, some of the tenants are not able to exist."

The land on the mountain was so poor; the soil so thin that it was incapable of producing crop of either quality or quantity. The settlers that the scheme was designed to support could scarcely exist, and the winters were unbearable. A local ballad stated,

> *Where moorfowl were plenty*
> *And hares made their den,*
> *T'was a wild habitation*
> *For Crommelin's white men.*

Nicholas Crommelin believed that his project would be a guaranteed success when he discovered iron ore near the village in 1843. He invested more money in other enterprises including the construction of a crude smelter to be heated with peat. The project failed due to a combination of low grade iron ore and an inadequate furnace.

Other entrepreneurs, who realised the importance of the iron ore, had better luck in the development of their schemes. The ore from this area was of a poor grade, full of impurities, and proved only to be useful when mixed with higher grade ore. The only benefit mining in the Cargan

Looking towards Trostan

area had over ore from elsewhere was that it was cheaper to extract. The need for iron ore began to decrease in the late 1800's, with most of the mines closing in the early 1900's and all by the 1920's. Some of the mines managed to sur-

Trostan

Leaving Newtown-Crommelin the number of occupied houses and farms diminishes; ruins and empty buildings become more obvious. They pay mute testimony to the failure of Nicholas Crommelins' experiment. It is true that rural depopulation has been a major problem in the Glens, but this road out of Newtown-Crommelin to Glenaan had more than its share. Lieutenant Greatorex points out in his account;

"The produce in potatoes, oats and flax is so uncertain from the state of the climate, against which nothing can prevail here, that tenant after tenant have abandoned their holdings and left their huts to go to ruin".

The road runs in a straight line for several miles along the back of Trostan. Trostan, standing at five hundred and fifty metres, is the highest point in County Antrim. The ascent of its slopes can initially be a slog over boggy ground, but the views from the top are well worth the effort. The top of Trostan is flat and surprisingly wide. There are some outcrops of peat, but the grey and rocky surface is not unlike a lunar landscape. The triangulation point rests on a high mound of rock, and is clearly visible from far off. From the summit, Lurigedan, Glenballyemon, Tievebulliagh and the coast of Scotland are all immediately recognisable. However on misty days, the sense of isolation can be quite unnerving.

vive longer by mining bauxite, an ingredient used in the production of aluminium, but again poor quality ore limited development. Bauxite mining ended for the most part in the 1930's, but Skerry Hill mine had a short resurgence during World War II.

The road now descends gently along the upper reaches of the Glendun river, flanked on the left side by Slieveanorra wood, an extensive expanse of coniferous forest. The river gets its name from the peat bog through which it flows. 'Dun' in Irish means 'brown' and as the rainwater percolates through the peat and into the river, it gets stained with the dark colour of the bog.

On the left stand the broad slopes of Orra Mountain, where the McQuillans and the McDonnells fought a decisive battle in 1558. The McQuillans had cavalry provided by their allies the O'Neills and they held the upper ground. In the face of these disadvantages McDonnells used guile, and tactical thinking. They dug deep pits in the bogland in front of their position by dead of night and concealed them with mats of rushes. The O'Neill cavalry charged the McDonnell position and foundered in the traps set for them. They were easy prey and the McQuillans were easily routed. From then on, the McDonnells held power in the Glens.

Bryvore Bridge, stands at a cross-

Orra Mountain

– 69 –

Cushendall & the Curfew Tower

roads. At this point Glendun and Glenaan meet. Take the road to the right that goes past the sheep pens. The road climbs briefly before levelling out through a worked peat bog area; and from there on its downhill all the way to Cushendall.

Rathlin Island

The crossing from Ballycastle to Rathlin is one of the most spectacular boat journeys in Ireland. The public ferry, more like a World War II landing craft than a ferry, takes approximately 45 minutes to make a journey that provides wonderful views of much of the North Coast. Fair Head dominates the views on the outward trip. The cliffs appear sheer and uninviting from the sea. This is actually one of the foremost rock climbing sites in Ireland, and many travel from all over the country to try their skills on its broad face. Soon the leisurely pace of the ferry pulls it away from the cliffs and it heads out into Rathlin Sound. In rough weather, this narrow sound has few equals. The tides that round the

The Rathlin Ferry at Ballycastle

Rathlin Island, from a distance

North coast and those sweeping up the Irish Sea meet in a boiling race that can be plainly seen on the calmest of days. In Irish it was known as Sloch na Marra, - 'the swallow of the sea'- an awesome title. It was also known as Coire Breacain, 'Breacain's Cauldron' named after the legendary sea raider whose fleet of fifty curraghs was swamped by the turbulence. This stretch of water has claimed many ships over the years, with over forty known wrecks recorded. The sea bed is littered with sunken ships and consequently it is abundant in marine life and is popular with divers. Small dingys and boats can be regularly seen taking people out to the sites of the wrecks.

Edwin Waugh, a traveller and writer, visited Rathlin in the Autumn of 1869. He observed that, *"the weather is generally milder there than it is on the mainland. Fogs, however are very prevalent in Rathlin....and these fogs are sometimes so dense as to render the island completely invisible even at a short distance. Hence vessels were often exposed to great danger in approaching this rocky isle, before the two lighthouses were erected upon it; and shipwrecks, from which none survived to tell the tale frequently took place upon its shores."*

The most famous wreck off Rathlin is the H.M.S. Drake which sank in Church Bay in October 17th 1917 after being hit by torpedoes from a German U-boat. The Drake, a four funnelled armoured cruiser was actually hit further out to sea while returning from protecting a west bound convoy. The captain, realising his ship could still manoeuvre, decided to make for the safety of the bay where he could hopefully beach his command. The Drake reached Church Bay at noon. However, shortly after reaching the safety of the harbour, the ship began to list rapidly and had to be abandoned. She sank nose first and now sits on the bottom of the bay with her stern only eighteen feet below the waves. The site of the Drake is marked by a buoy, but even with this precaution at least three ships have got into difficulties as a result of hitting the submerged hulk. It has been said that some islanders made good from the wreck of the Drake. As a warship she carried munitions, and cordite was regularly washed up on the Rathlin beaches. Those islanders recognised a use for these cordite sticks and apparently for a long time used them as a kind of fire lighter.

Rathlin begins to dominate the near horizon like some sea fortress with it's high cliffs and rocky shoreline. On a good day, the island is picturesque and inviting. In bad weather, the white cliffs look grey and menacing and there have been times when the island was cut off from the mainland by high seas and gale force winds. The first lighthouse to be seen is called South Lighthouse. It stands at sea level on Rue Point. From here, the cliffs climb steeply and it is difficult for the first time passenger to see anywhere that the ferry might safely dock. Eventually, Church Bay is reached and the harbour becomes visible. The port itself is surrounded by thick walls needed to keep boats safe from the punishing effects of the winter seas. It is common enough for Rathlin to be completely isolated from Ballycastle during storms and the remoteness of this island is easily appreciated. However, it is this very remoteness which enhances Rathlins appeal, in addition to the abundance of its animal and bird life.

Rathlin has a history in keeping with its strategic location. Ptolemy and Pliny called it Ricina. The Norsemen were regular visitors and it is believed to have been descended upon by the Viking warriors sailing North after their defeat at the battle of Clontarf at the hands of the Irish king, Brian Boru. In 1216 King John granted Rathlin to the Earl of Galloway and it was subsequently seized by the Bissetts who settled in Glenarm. It has of course its famous connection with Robert the Bruce who took refuge there and who, according to legend, took heart from the persistence of that six times baffled spider.

Rathlin has also had its share of infamy. In 1575, the Earl of Essex, at one time the much beloved favourite of Elizabeth I learned in Carrickfergus that his old enemy Sorley Boy McDonnell had sent his women, children and valuables to the island for safety. Sorley was within the relative security of the Glens. Essex sent an expedition comprising three frigates and a force of soldiers to Rathlin. One of the ship captains was Francis Drake. The expedition landed and made light work of any resistance offered by the 'castle' on the island. Sir Henry Sidney wrote, *"There have been slain that came out of the castle of all sorts two hundred. They be occupied still in the killing and have slain all that they have found in caves and in the cliffs of the sea to the number of 300 or 400 more."*

Essex of course penned to Elizabeth an appropriate description of the events on Rathlin. The site of the massacre is known as Crocknascridlin, 'the hill of the screaming.'

In 1642 after the Irish rebellion had broken out, a force of Campbells landed on the island. Their traditional enemies the McDonnells were by then the recognised rulers of Rathlin. The 1200 strong force went to work with a will, and a massacre was the result. Local tradition reports that women and children were tossed from the high cliffs into the sea at a spot called Sloaknacailly, 'the hags' pit'.

For those who wonder as to whether Rathlin is Irish or Scots in identity, it might be useful to know that Edwin

Waugh had two relevant items of information to report. In 1797, every male adult on the island, with the exception of the parish priest and another 'gentleman' took the test of allegiance to the United Irishmen, and almost all the islanders spoke Irish as their first language.

From the harbour at Church Bay there are two walks of reasonable distance, ending at the lighthouse at Bull point to the West and at Rue point in the South. For the visitors looking for a short stroll, or with spare time on their hands, the road to East Lighthouse provides an alternative with its fantastic views of the Scottish coastline, and in particular, of the Mull of Kintyre. This Lighthouse was the site of some of Marconi's experiments with radio communication. He used the site, and one in Ballycastle, to perfect the method of 'wireless technology' which he had patented in 1896, and he managed to send his first transmission between the two sites in 1898. The aim of the work, was not only to perfect his 'wireless technology' but to provide Lloyds of London with an account of the ships that used the sea lanes around the island.

A choppy sea at Rue Point

Church Bay

The island is dotted with ruins dating back as far as Neolithic times, although there is proof of human habitation as far back as the Mesolithic period. In the eighteenth century, Rathlin had a population of some 1200. One of the most recent buildings going to ruin, is the Kelp Store that stands on Mill Bay. This building, constructed out of limestone blocks, was built to house one of Rathlin's main exports – kelp. The kelp was made by burning seaweed in large kilns, with the resulting ash being kept in the store until a ship was sent to collect it. The kelp was then used on the mainland for the bleaching of linen, and later for the production of iodine.

Once off the boat, take the road to the right, passing by the Manor House. This was built in 1760 by Robert Gage, son of Reverend John Gage who bought the lease for the entire island in 1746 from the Earl of Antrim for the grand sum of £1,750. The building is still in use, but today it provides accommodation for visitors to the island. Go past the pub, a good stop for lunch, and keep an eye on the harbour for signs of one of the islands permanent seal colonies. At the far end of the harbour is the islands visitors centre, with full information on the island's history.

Although these walks on Rathlin take place on roads, traffic is never a worry. The island only has approximately seventy five people living on it at present and consequently there are few cars. The silence is only broken by the sounds of the sea and the birds, so any oncoming car is soon heard. There is a sense of being suspended in time, and any of the small roads on Rathlin will soon take you away from the sounds and images we associate with modern day living.

Seals resting by the shore

These small Rathlin fields were once associated with a breed of horse called the Rahery. It was used throughout the North of Ireland as a working animal, for although it was small it was sturdy. The Statistical Survey of Co. Monaghan praised the Rahery horse and added that they were *"extremely cheap, seldom exceeding three guineas in price.....most durable and serviceable, well calculated for a hilly country and they live to great age."* The Rahery horses were possibly a variety of the strain known as the Cushendall pony, a breed once very popular on farms throughout the nearby Glens.

The route leaves the main area of habitation around Church Bay and the road undulates through fields and a series of four small loughs. These fresh water loughs with their marsh banks, provide an appropriate habitat for much of Rathlin's bird population. Snipe and Bunting thrive on the marsh land, while Grebe, Moorhens, Coots and Ducks can be found on the loughs themselves. The local farmers adopt farming methods which help to encourage bird life rather than destroy it. These methods may not be the most financially rewarding but the island people show great respect for and awareness of the needs of the wildlife inhabiting their island.

Eventually the walker arrives at the open flat land that marks Rue Point. There is an automatic lighthouse here and also an old ruined building. This area is home to a large seal colony and at low tide in warm weather, the seals can be seen basking on the rocks. They seem to show little fear of visitors and will allow the quiet observer to get quite close before they decide to retreat to the safety of the water. They are a very inquisitive animal and will watch the visitor as much as they themselves are observed.

The old building is known locally as the 'smugglers house'. Rathlin was a centre for smuggling in the early 1800's with lace, tobacco and alcohol being the main items for barter. The smuggling trade was tackled in 1821 when the then head of the Gage family, Robert, moved coast-guards onto the island. He also arranged for this natural harbour, known locally as Ushet Port, to be blocked with boulders, thereby making Church Bay the only available place at which to land boats in safety.

The more rugged and hilly landscape to the north dominates the skyline. The long line of white limestone cliffs leading to Bull Point is visible. It is over this landscape that the walker will travel to the West Lighthouse.

Instead of turning right from the boat, turn to the left and the road quickly brings you to St. Thomas' Church of Ireland. This church is reported to have been built on the ruins of one of Rathlin Island's original churches. History relates that two churches were established on Rathlin by early Christians – Saint Comgall established one in 580 A.D. and the other was founded in 630 A.D. by Sigenius. The great Columba also landed in Rathlin and founded a religious house which flourished for almost three centuries until it was destroyed by the Vikings in 973, when they also killed the abbot.

The road rises above the Bay and provides dramatic views of the small settlements below as well as of Rue Point, Fair Head, and Knocklayde Mountain. To the north the landscape is marred by the tall wind generators that finally provided the local islanders with mains electricity. They are named after the children of Lir, who after being turned to swans by a cruel spell were destined to spend hundreds of years on the sea of Moyle surrounding Rathlin. The story tells how Finnoula, frightened that the children should be separated by the winter storms that sweep across this stretch of water, arranged for the children to gather at Carricknarone on the north of the island.

The road leads down into a series of hollows and climbs again, and with each rise in the road more of the coastline of North Antrim comes into view, depending of course on the prevailing conditions. The landscape in time undergoes

The Church of Ireland, Rathlin

Lighthouse a woodland appears seemingly out of nowhere. This is Kinramer Wood, a plantation of stunted trees that seem to be battling for survival. From here it is only another twenty minutes walking until the West Lighthouse is reached.

This lighthouse, known also as Bull Lighthouse is a curiosity in itself. It was built high up in the cliffs and is a considerable feat of engineering. It was completed in 1919. Tons of rock had to be blasted from the cliff to make a shelf for the lighthouse

Rathlin Sound & Fairhead

a dramatic change. One feature of Rathlin is it's shortage of trees. The severity of the weather and the exposed position limits their growth. However as the walker nears the West to stand on. Since the cliffs were so high the designer was worried that the light on top of the tower might be obscured by the fog and mist that regularly envelopes the

headland. To overcome this problem, the light has been placed on the bottom of the rocky shelf with the keepers house standing behind and above.

The Royal Society for the Protection of Birds have an agreement with the Commissioners of Irish Lights, who own the lighthouse, to use the viewing platform from April to August. The area around the west tip of the island is a nature reserve managed by the R.S.P.B. and access is restricted. It is possible however to organise a visit to the lighthouse by contacting R.S.P.B. staff. The view is breathtaking and especially so during the months of May and June when the breeding season for the visiting birds is at it's height. The sight of thousands of birds occupying every solitary space

on the rocks and sea stacks is unforgettable. The scene from this vantage point must be one of the most incredible and enduring, not only in the North Antrim area but in all of Ireland.

The range of birds visiting these towering cliffs is impressive. Guillemots, Kittiwakes, Fulmars and brightly coloured Puffins vie for space, landing precariously on small ledges with food for their young. Relatively rare birds also visit Rathlin during this time including Gannets and Skuas. Sometimes, above the breeding sites, birds of prey such as Buzzards can be seen waiting to steal unprotected chicks. The Warden of this unique reserve lives on the island and can provide information about the birds in the various colonies.

The return to the harbour is by way of the same road, though for those feeling particularly tired after the days exertions, there is a bus that runs to and from

the Lighthouse during the summer months. The return journey however is worth making on foot. It is worth noting that Rathlin also provides a haven for many wild flowers. The walker can so be taken with the views that the wild rare flowers that line the roadways are missed, but throughout the journey in either direction the walker can hear the same sound that Waugh heard back in 1869 when he poetically described how,

"the moan of the sea on Rathlin's rocky shore
came wild upon the ear."

Dusk and a sea trip home, the shipwreck buoy.

Giant's Causeway to Dunseverick

T he Giant's Causeway is sometimes referred to as the eighth wonder of the world. That is very much a matter of opinion but as a marketing ploy it has been very successful. They come from all over the world to see the Causeway, just as they have been for centuries. In its early days as a tourist attraction, the whole area was difficult to access, and writer upon writer described the various tribulations he had to endure on the journey. Nowadays of course its a different story. The Causeway is Northern Irelands biggest single tourist attraction and the site is well catered for in every respect. The track between the Giant's Causeway and the ruins of Dunseverick Castle some 7 miles away is well sign posted. Moreover, it is a marvellous walk in every respect and easy to complete.

The cliff pathway follows the contours of the coast but in order to visit the actual Causeway you must take the path leading down to the shore and after that, you can ascend the steps on the other side that lead to the cliff path again and then proceed on to Dunseverick. Alternatively of course you can return to the car park and so make the walk much shorter.

The Causeway is a huge ongoing attraction, as the steady stream of visitors going to and coming from it will testify.

The Causeway

Few however will bother to chronicle their impression of the place, in the detailed way that many did in the past. It could be called a 'recent' tourist attraction, for it isn't mentioned in the Annals of the Four Masters and it doesn't merit inclusion in any of the maps of the 16th and 17th centuries. That is not surprising given the inaccessibility of the locality in those days and its location in what would have been considered a remote corner of Ireland. Nothing was written about it until the late 17th century when there was an upsurge in scientific interest and as a result several papers were written describing its wonders. Some were of dubious value; written by people like Sir Richard Buckley who had never properly seen the place. He observed it from the cliff top and wrote,

"The Coast is a very great height from the sea, but rising gradually on the landslide to the edge of the precipice, it is all covered over with an excellent sweet grass: when you come to the precipice, there is no going down there it is so precipitously steep, but with much Labour and some hazard it may be climbed up...."

Opinions differed in the 18th century as to the origins of the Causeway. A folk tale suggested that it had been constructed by the legendary Fionn McCool to allow him easy access to Scotland where he was having an on going feud with a giant as well proportioned as himself. There are place names associated with the Irish giant everywhere -

Mist over the Causeway

The Giant's Loom, Giant's Organ, Giant's Chimney, Giant's Well, Giant's Boot. There were two schools of scientific thought as to how it originated, - Neptunists and Vulcanists. One was convinced that the basalt from which the Causeway was built had been deposited by the sea. The other argued that it resulted from volcanic activity.

It was a Frenchman, Demarest, who first argued that the basalt was volcanic in origin. However, like most theorists of the time, he had never visited the site, and his conclusions were made from drawings. There were of course stones from the Causeway circulating here and there. It was not unknown for piles of basalt rock to be hewn out of the Causeway, loaded on board a small ship and taken away, for both scientific and decorative purposes. Tons of basalt were hauled away by cart to decorate gardens. A potential scavenger was the novelist Sir Walter Scott who viewed the stones and pillars from the sea. He was touring various nautical sights by boat at the behest of a Mr Stevenson, a Senior Commissioner of Lights and grandfather of another writer, Robert Louis Stevenson. Scott, who was lame, didn't land on the Causeway, but he later wrote that had he not had a severe headache on the day, he would have selected four columns to be hauled on board to decorate the porch of his majestic home in Scotland.

The Earl of Bristol, Bishop of Derry who lived on the other side of the River Bann had a roadway built down to the Causeway in the late 18th century, by which time its fame was on the increase. The great Dr Johnson the lexicographer however was not convinced. His associate Boswell prevailed upon him to visit Ireland. The great man responded *"It is the last place on earth where I should wish to travel"* and when Boswell suggested he might visit the Causeway, Johnson made his famous judgment, that whereas, *"it might well be worth seeing, it was not worth going to see"*. He never bothered to go.

His opinion however must be weighed against that of the society lady and avid traveller Mrs Delaney who in the 18th century travelled there in her horse-drawn carriage. She pronounced it to be *"the most wondrous sight that is perhaps to be seen in the world."*

I have no idea as to how much of the wider world the same Mrs Delaney had seen. Another less affluent 18th century traveller, the impecunious Chevalier De La Tocnaye was also impressed by what he saw and observed that even his horse was *"enchanted by the beauty of the prospect."*

The Causeway became a practical proposition for the ordinary tourist with the opening up of the Antrim Coast Road in 1837. Before long it was as popular as Killarney, and as the numbers of tourists increased so too did the throngs of hawkers, beggars, sellers of souvenirs, ballad mongers, and guides all hoping to eke out a living. The harassment they caused was a regular source of complaint among visitors in the 19th century. Most writers made unfavourable mention of the guides and boatmen who crowded around them. The novelist Thackeray was terrified

Causeway visitor

by them. He was man-handled into a small boat and taken out to sea for a boat trip that was thoroughly unpleasant due to the rough sea that was running at the time. Thackeray was far from impressed and commented unfavourably on his visit,

"The solitude is awful....it looks like the beginning of the world; the sea looks older than in other places, the hills and the rocks strange....a remnant of chaos...well I am a Cockney. I wish I were in Pall Mall......Mon Dieu! and I have travelled a hundred miles to see that?"

By the late 19th century the Giant's Causeway was a hive of tourist activity. The nearby town of Portrush was a popular holiday resort and people of every age and background were heading out to see what was by now being hailed as a wonder of the world. A steady stream of jaunting cars plied to and from Portrush in all kinds of weather. The electric tramway that began in 1891 made the place even more accessible. It ran from Portrush to Bushmills and then on to the Causeway. It was the earliest example of hydro-electric powered transport in the British Isles. By that time the name of the Causeway was firmly established in the imagination of the world at large.

The narrow road running down to the Causeway takes you past a large outcrop on the left called the Great Stookan. It follows the line of the shore round Port Ganny and leads directly to the most popular part of the Causeway. The route follows the one taken by Mrs Delaney and all those other well-known vistors. No matter what has been said the site is impressive. Somewhere in the region of 40,000 columns of dark basalt rock, mostly hexagonal, and formed from volcanic lava some 60 million years ago, march to meet the sea. The footpath continues on through the Giant's Gate round another bay called Port Noffer. A large boulder lies among the rocks. It's known as the Giant's Boot, and a little way further on stand the vertical 'pipes' of what is known as the Giant's Organ.

The route now rises in a series of steps just before the Organ - 162 in all – to the cliff path which leads you on towards Dunseverick. The path winds along the top of the headland, skirts Port na Spaniagh, and a small low lying headland called Lacada Point. It is worth stopping here a

Clockwise from top left: Climbing the Causeway, The Giant's Organ, Wild flowers don't care were they grow, The Giant's Boot.

Looking East

while and reflecting back some four hundred years to the year 1588.

In October that year the flagship Girona, pride of the Armada, left the shelter of Killybegs Harbour in South West Donegal where she had put in for repairs. Her initial objective was a safe return to Spain, but that was not practical for the moment and so she was heading for relative safety in Scotland. She was severely overloaded, carrying between 1300 and 1500 men instead of the normal 550 and to add to her troubles she had a faulty rudder and was taking water. Rounding the North Coast of Antrim proved too much of a challenge that stormy Autumn. The Girona was lifted, driven and skewered on to the rocks of Lacada Point where she was smashed and pounded by heavy seas on October 28th 1588 until she sank below the dark waters of Port na Spaniagh. Of the thirteen hundred or so men on board only about five survived. The bodies of the dead who were washed ashore were apparently buried among the rocks above the high water mark.

The path to Dunseverick

Her whereabouts and that of the treasure she carried remained one of Europe's great maritime mysteries until 1968, when what little remained of the wreckage was discovered by marine archaeologist Robert Stenuit. He had been searching the North coast for years hoping to find the Girona and her treasure. He initially followed the evidence provided by reports written at the time which stated that the ship, *"struck hard against the rock of Bunboyes......this rock is hard by Sorley Boy's house."* Bunboyes is the old Gaelic place name given to the mouth of the River Bush. Sorley Boy occupied Dunluce Castle and both sites are further to the North. However, the Ordnance Survey Memoirs of 1835, normally very reliable, reported how it was said locally that a ship of the Armada had actually fired shot at the Giant's Chimney in the mistaken belief that it was Dunluce Castle. Whether that shot was an act of aggression or a call for help isn't clear, but the Chimney is right beside Port na Spaniagh and Lacada Point and so it is probable that the Girona was heading for disaster and was signalling its plight.

Stenuit spent hundreds of hours diving and exploring the seabed at various possible sites. Local folklore finally provided the answer. Port na Spaniagh translates roughly as the 'The Spaniards' Bay' and the name contained the answer to Stenuits' quest. History hadn't marked the place of drowning. The folk memory and the place name preserved its location for posterity. Looking down on that place of drowning, it is easy to picture the terror that confronted the men on board when through the storm and the night they dimly saw the high cliffs looming above them as they were driven helplessly onto the reef that claimed their ship. The treasure recovered by Stenuit is now in the Girona Room of the Ulster Museum in Belfast. Among the many

Lacada Point

beautiful exhibits there is a small gold ring with a poignant message inscribed 'No tengo mas que dar te.' It is a coded statement of love. It means 'I have nothing more to give you.'

The path to Dunseverick continues along the cliff tops. The views on a clear day are glorious and the walk is far from demanding. It undulates gently round promontories and the craggy Benbane Head, the most Northerly point in County Antrim. Then there is another series of cliffs and once past a headland called Portnagovna, the track descends gently towards Dunseverick.

The ruins of Dunseverick Castle stand on a grassy knoll overlooking the sea. Little remains of it, for like so many ancient buildings of its kind throughout Ireland, the centuries and the weather have taken their toll. Dunseverick looks forlorn and uncared for,

Dunseverick Castle

and the manner in which it is outlined against the sea and the sky accentuates its isolation. On closer inspection it should become apparent that its location was for purposes of defence, with steep cliffs on the seaward side and a narrow causeway on the other. Nowadays it is hard to imagine that Dunseverick was once looked upon as a place of importance, - a centre of authority and power in the ancient Kingdom of Dalriada, which spanned the Sea of

is much older. It is just one of several which serve to remind us that this remote and beautiful corner of North Antrim played an important role in the early history of the North.

Dunseverick

Moyle embracing both part of Argyle and part of Antrim. There is a strong tradition which claims that Dunseverick lay at the end of one of the five great routes leading from Tara, a story which would enhance its claim to being a site of early importance. Though the stone ruins of the building probably date from Elizabethan times, the original site

Charles McAuley

Charles McAuley was my uncle and the youngest of a family of eight - four boys and four girls. He was born in 1910 and reared on a farm. He followed his brothers and sisters to Glenaan School where he showed an early aptitude for art. Even as a child he was forever drawing and painting the life of the farm and the surrounding country-side in Glenaan, Glencorp and Glendun, so it was no surprise when he chose the precarious life of a professional painter. He studied for a short while in Belfast and at the Glasgow College of Art, but the pull of the Glens was too strong and he chose to abandon study and return to where his heart already lay.

Charles as a young man

He married my aunt Peggy (O'Loan), a native of Cushendall and he set up a small studio in Shore Street. Cushendall was to be his home for the rest of his long life, in preference to Belfast or Ballymena where there was a larger more prosperous buying public. Charles knew the professional cost of remaining in the Antrim Glens, especially in the hungry thirties when he began his career, but city life was not for him, and the large towns made him uneasy. He was a Glensman and he knew it.

The river at Lubitavish & the old Glenaan mill

couldn't afford proper canvas, he painted on board. When war broke out, he painted on tea chests and there were times when he struggled to make a living, but he kept on working, observing, developing. He painted life on the small farms when lint was pulled, hay lapped and stooked with rake and fork, turf drawn from the mountain by horse and on slide car, cows milked in dim byres lit with oil lamps. He painted the scenery and the seasons, the rivers and the mountain roads where passing neighbours always found time to stop and talk *"about the weather's way, the law on catch dams and the price of hay."*

So, the Glens became his subject matter. He loved and he knew it all intimately, - the hills, the valleys, the shore, the men and women who were his friends and his neighbours. He painted life in the Glens as he saw and understood it. He painted the familiar, and he celebrated his acute sense of place in oil and watercolour. In the early days when he

He missed the old ways and whenever he had to leave Cushendall for any length of time, he missed it as well and would be impatient to get back home. If ever a man could be described as being rooted in his own place, that man was Charles McAuley. In 1989, I made a short film about his life and work for the Education Department of the BBC. At the close of filming he stood by the banks of the Glendun River, close to the graveyard where his par-

Glendun

The house by the river

Cottage below Tievebulliagh

The White Mare

ents and his brothers Bernard and Francis were buried and in simple but heartfelt words he let it be known that the Antrim Glens meant everything to him and that his fondest wish was that he would live out the remainder of his life in the place that was so dear to his heart. He had his wish. In September 1999 at the age of 89 he died and was buried among his own people in the churchyard in Cushendall.

The Slide Car

Dear Reader

We hope you have enjoyed this book. It is the second book in our walking series
following on from 'Bernard Davey's Mourne'

For a more relaxed appreciation of Ireland we also publish a range of illustrated titles :–

Cottage
Publications

Cottage Publications
15 Ballyhay Road
Donaghadee, Co. Down
N. Ireland, BT21 0NG

Strangford Shores	Donegal Highlands
Dundalk & North Louth	Drogheda & the Boyne Valley
Armagh	The Mournes
Belfast	Fermanagh
Antrim, town & country	Omagh
Inishowen	South Donegal
The Heart of Down	

Also available in our 'Illustrated History & Companion' Range are:-

Coleraine and the Causeway Coast	City of Derry
Lisburn	Banbridge
Ballymoney	Holywood

We can also supply prints, individually signed by the artist, of the paintings featured in
the above titles as well as many other areas of Ireland.

For more details on these superb publications and to view samples of the paintings they
contain, you can visit our web site at **www.cottage-publications.com** or alternatively
you can contact us as follows:-

Telephone: +44 (028) 9188 8033   Fax: +44 (028) 9188 8063